PINOT NOIR
MERLOT
BORDEAUX
RIESLING
GRIGIO
ZINFANDEL
LBEC
GEWÜRZTRAMINER
MUSCAT
ROUSSANNE
SYRAH
Viognier
SHERRY
CABERNET
GAMAY
BURGUNDY
semillon
PROSECCO
PORT
ROSE
SHIRAZ
Chenin Blanc
NNAY

PINOT NOIR

MERLOT

BORDEAUX

PINOT GRIGIO

RIESLING

ZINFANDEL

GEWÜRZTRAMINER

MUSCAT

ROUSSANNE

Viognier

SYRAH

SHERRY

MALBEC

CABERNET

GAMAY

BURGUNDY

PROSECCO

PORT

ROSE

sémillon

CHARDONNAY

SHIRAZ

Chenin Blanc

THIS

JOURNAL

★ belongs to ★

....

WINE IS BOTTLED POETRY.

—Robert Louis Stevenson

POTTER STYLE
DESIGN BY LAURA PALESE

Reference text by Barrie Cleveland, publisher of the independent winery direc-
tory website California Winery Advisor, www.CaliforniaWineryAdvisor.com.

Copyright © 2010 by Potter Style. Published by Potter Style, an imprint of the
Crown Publishing Group, a division of Random House, Inc., New York.

www.clarksonpotter.com
Printed in China
ISBN 978-0-307-59132-6

★ YOUR ★
oenofILE

Pour a glass, take a sip, then take some notes in this journal—the essential companion for wine lovers.

Vino Journal provides plenty of pages for writing about the wines you buy, taste, and serve. Record the details about each wine (the name, varietal, region, vintage, price) so you'll remember what to order or buy in the future. Make sure to jot down a few comments about the color, nose, and taste of each wine as well (you can use the glossary of wine terms in this journal for inspiration). Feel free to write down specific information like where you were when you sampled the wine (a restaurant? a vineyard? a friend's home?) or what you ate with the wine and if it was a pleasing match. Plenty of reference information appears in this journal for rounding out your knowledge, including descriptions of various grape varietals, recommended food and wine pairings, and classic cheese and wine combinations. In the back of this journal you'll also find a list of notable wine blogs and websites worth visiting.

Happy tasting!

GeTTiNG

★ the most from a ★

BoTTLE
of WiNE

Tasting wine can be a fun, educational, and even enlightening
experience. With a few techniques and ideas of what to look and
taste for, wine can be much more than fermented grape juice. There
are four steps to tasting wine, and each step should be a deliberate
process. In a large tulip-shaped glass, pour yourself a small
sample of wine and follow these steps.

APPEARANCE: Check the color and clarity of the wine. The wine should be brilliant and not cloudy. Tilt your glass and look down on the wine against a white background. As wines age, the color of the wine will change. White wines become yellow and may show a tint of brown along the edges of the glass. This will prepare you for a wine that has mellowed and perhaps is not as fruity as it once was. Red wines lose color and look brickish, which may indicate the wine will no longer have its youthful vigor. Instead it may be well-aged, with softer tannins and more complex flavors.

SMELL, AROMA, OR "THE NOSE": The aroma of the wine is a very important factor since we are able to perceive more flavors and nuances with our nose than we can with our palate. To get the most out of the tasting, swirl your glass to aerate the wine and allow the juice to coat the sides of the glass. Then get your nose into the glass and smell. With this technique the aromas from the wine will be concentrated and easier to discern and enjoy. In white wines find the fruit, floral, grassy, mineral, clove, and perhaps wood aromas. For red wines, you may discover spice, nuts, mint, earthy flavors, leather, blueberries, and oak.

TASTE: The palate picks up sweet, sour, salty, and bitter components. Be sure to move the wine around your mouth to get the full tactile sensation of the acids, sweetness, and tannins. To enjoy the aromatic components of the wine, take in a little air through your mouth, and with a slight gargling sound, you get the full impact of the wine. Enjoy the complexity of these sensations and look for flavors of pepper, plums, perfume, tar, cinnamon, bell peppers, and chocolate.

AFTERTASTE: A good wine has a lingering and well-balanced aftertaste. Some wines may have a strong or sharp aftertaste of acidity or intense wood flavors, or no aftertaste at all. If the wine is made well, from quality fruit, it will have long, lingering aromas and nuances that are in harmony.

WINE GRAPE
VaRIeTIES
★ overview ★

Use this guide to explore the various grape flavor profiles. Some wines may have many flavor elements, and—sadly—some will have few.

POPULAR WHITE WINE GRAPE VARIETIES

GRAPE	TASTING NOTES
CHARDONNAY	Round and viscous with pear, green apple, peach, tropical fruit, citrus, mineral, flinty, subtle spice, and butterscotch flavors. Notes of butter, toasted oak, vanilla, and coconut with oak aging or barrel fermentation. If wine goes through malolactic fermentation, concentrated butter, cream, and even hazelnut flavors can emerge. Generally full-bodied and dry.
CHENIN BLANC	Melon, honeydew, honeysuckle, cantaloupe, quince, grass, hay. Can have floral, mineral, or herbal qualities. Made dry, off-dry, or sweet.
FRENCH COLOMBARD	Bright, sometimes spicy with melon and pine-apple flavors. Made dry or off-dry, and found in white table wine blends.

GRAPE	TASTING NOTES
GEWÜRZTRAMINER	Mandarin orange, gardenia, honeysuckle, mango, apple, spices, nutmeg, and ginger. This wine can have a floral perfume and rose petal quality. Made dry, off-dry, or sweet.
MARSANNE	In the same way Sémillon adds weight to Sauvignon Blanc, Marsanne is frequently paired up with Roussanne to make blended white wines in the Rhône Valley and in California. Wines made from Marsanne can display aromas of nuts and vegetables and show a softer acidity than Roussanne.
MUSCAT	The grapey, floral, orange-blossom scent of Muscat is easy to remember after only one whiff. Most of the wines range from sweet to intensely sweet and make a lovely complement to fresh berries on a summer evening.
PINOT BLANC	Apple, nut, almond, fruit, oak; medium-body, with a round, creamy texture and often a bit of spice. Malolactic fermentation can create notes of butter, cream, and hazelnut. Usually made dry. Often aged in oak, adding vanilla, smoke, and occasionally tar components.

GRAPE	TASTING NOTES
PINOT GRIS/ PINOT GRIGIO	Melon, lemon, apple, pear, citrus, light honey, ginger, and tropical fruit flavors. Made dry to off-dry. When aged in oak, the wine can have notes of vanilla, almond, and smoke.
RIESLING	Apple, pear, peach, apricot, floral, rose petal, and violet. Can develop a mineral, flinty flavor. Made dry, off-dry, or sweet.
ROUSSANNE	From France's Rhône Valley, this grape produces floral aromatic wines with mineral flavors and refreshing acidity. It is frequently blended with Marsanne in its native France.
SAUVIGNON BLANC (FUMÉ BLANC)	Fig, honeydew, citrus, grass, grapefruit, lime, melon, bell pepper, green olive, and asparagus flavors. When aged or fermented in oak, the wine can have a smoky bouquet. Crisp, light, and dry.

GRAPE	TASTING NOTES
SCHEUREBE	Scheurebe (shoy-ray-beh) is a rare grape variety found in the Pfalz, Rheinhessen, and Nahe regions of Germany. Small blocks of Scheurebe can be found in Napa Valley, Virginia, southern Ontario, and on a very small scale in British Columbia. The wines have a full-body, pronounced crisp acidity, lots of fruit, and a bouquet and taste reminiscent of black currants.
SÉMILLON	Possessing an almost unctuous texture, the thick quality of Sémillon makes a great partner to the acidity of Sauvignon Blanc. The two grapes often team up to produce extraordinary dessert wines that hit high notes with fruit tarts and crème caramel.
VIOGNIER	In the vineyard, yields and acid levels tend to be low and the grape is susceptible to disease and rot. In the winery, it is very temperamental. But once in the bottle or the glass, a well-made Viognier comes with a deep yellow color and an exquisite, exotic bouquet of apricots, tropical fruit, honeysuckle, ripe peaches, mango, pear, pineapple, guava, kiwi, and tangerine. Light- to medium-bodied, made dry or off-dry, with some made sweet from late-harvested fruit.

POPULAR RED WINE GRAPE VARIETIES

GRAPE	TASTING NOTES
BARBERA	Blackberry, currants, ripe fruit, earth, and leather. Oak aging adds vanilla, smoke, toast, and coconut.
CABERNET FRANC	Raspberry, cherry, plum, strawberry, olive, black currant, herbs, violet, bell peppers, and smoke. Can develop mushroom, earth, cedar, cigar box flavors. Classically blended with Cabernet Sauvignon and Merlot. Made medium-to full-bodied, dry.
CABERNET SAUVIGNON	Jam, pepper, spice, berry flavors, black currant, cherry, chocolate, tobacco, nut, cinnamon, coffee, peppercorn, pimento, and plum. Can be herbaceous, with asparagus, bell pepper, and green olive. Can have notes of vanilla, coconut, smoke, and tar with oak aging. Bottle aging can provide cedar, cigar box, musk, mushroom, earth, and leather flavors. Full-bodied, dry.
CHARBONO	This grape usually produces very dark wines with distinctive aromas of plums along with pepper, leather, tar, and wild berry. The wines can be acidic with high tannin levels and can age five to ten (or more) years.

GRAPE	TASTING NOTES
CINSAULT	Strawberry, musk, and meat; floral, perfumed. Oak aging can add vanilla, smoke, toast, and tar. Made medium-bodied and dry.
DOLCETTO	Like Barbera, Dolcetto hails from the Piedmont region in northwest Italy. Though softer in acidity than Barbera, it can be more tannic and quite fruity.
GAMAY (VALDIGUIÉ)	Raspberry, strawberry, cherry, violet, rose petal, and spun sugar. Made off-dry or sweet. Much of the Gamay planted in California is not Gamay at all. Some has been found to be a clone of Pinot Noir.
GRENACHE NOIR	Probably the world's most widely planted red grape, largely in France and Spain. It needs devigorating soils where it can produce exquisite, luscious wines. Grenache is the basis for the great Southern Rhône blends, usually making up to 60 to 80 percent of the blend in both Châteauneuf du Pape and the Côtes du Rhône. Black currant, blackberry; dusty. Oak aging provides vanilla, smoke, toast, and tar. With aging tobacco, dried apricot, and cigar box notes.

GRAPE	TASTING NOTES
MALBEC	Plum, peppercorn, cherry, nut, tobacco, spice, and anise. Oak aging provides vanilla, smoke, and cedar. Aging adds cigar box, musk, mushroom, earth, and leather flavors. Full-bodied, dry.
MERLOT	Raspberry, blueberry, black cherry, plum, eucalyptus, bell pepper, nut, chocolate, clove, caramel, bay leaf, peppercorn, raisin, bell pepper, green olive, tobacco, and spice. Oak aging can add vanilla, coconut, smoke, and tar. Bottle aging develops truffle, mushroom, earth, coffee, leather, cedar, and cigar box. Velvety, soft, and dry.
MOURVÈDRE	Like Grenache, the Mourvèdre grape is probably Spanish in origin. Under the name Mataro—or no name at all—it has been part of California "field blends" for more than a century. It produces sturdy wines with good acid and, some astringency, and it can develop enticing blackberry aromas and flavors. Mourvèdre produces meaty, intense wines that age well. Rarely bottled alone, it goes into the better quality Southern Rhône blends where it adds a wildness and complexity to the wine.

GRAPE	TASTING NOTES
NEBBIOLO	This grape produces deep and demanding wines, with full tannins, acid, and general depth of flavor with hints of roses, cherries, raspberries, prunes, tobacco, and tar. The wine can age for many years, and the grape is one of the hardest to grow.
PETITE SIRAH	Grown mainly in California, this red wine grape was initially thought to be related to the renowned Syrah of France's Rhône region. Some, however, believe it is actually a variety called Durif which was also grown in the Rhône but is now almost extinct. Petite Sirah produces a robust, deep-colored wine with spice, plum, and peppery flavors that packs plenty of tannins and has good aging ability.
PINOT MEUNIER	It's like Pinot Noir, in a softer way. Lots of Pinot Meunier is grown in the north of France to make Champagne, and a few producers have embraced it in California. It makes wines light in color with good acidity and aromatic fruity flavors.

GRAPE	TASTING NOTES
PINOT NOIR	Bing cherry, strawberry, raspberry, ripe tomato, rose petal, spice, rosemary, cinnamon, caraway, peppermint, oregano, green tea, black olive, plum, and rhubarb. Notes of mushroom, earth, leather, meat, and truffle can also develop. Oak aging provides vanilla, coconut, smoke, cigar box, cedar, toast, and tar.
SANGIOVESE	Cherry, dark cherry, strawberry, blueberry, orange peel, plum, herb, bay leaf, cinnamon, clove, thyme, and violet. Vanilla, smoke, toast, and tar flavors are possible when aged in oak. Usually made dry.
SYRAH	A very dark and flavorful grape that is easy to work with. Healthy, early ripening, resistant to mildew and rot, suitable for winemaking in a variety of styles. Shiraz (Australian for Syrah) has a distinguished history Down Under, being the most widely planted grape in that country. Blackberry, pepper, plum, black currant, grass, black peppers, licorice, clove, thyme, bay leaf, herbal, sandalwood, musk, and earth. Oak aging provides vanilla, coconut, smoke, toast, and tar flavors. Aging can add cedar, cigar box, and leather. Made full-bodied, dry.

GRAPE	TASTING NOTES
ZINFANDEL	This grape produces robust red wine along with very popular semisweet rosé wines labeled White Zinfandel. Wines exhibit raspberry, blackberry, boysenberry, cranberry, black cherry, plum, licorice, spice, cinnamon, black pepper, and earth. Oak aging provides vanilla, coconut, smoke, and toast. Also made into late-harvest Port style wines. Aging offers tar, leather, mushroom, cedar, and cigar box flavors. Made full-bodied, dry.

WINE IS SUNLIGHT HELD TOGETHER BY WATER.

—GALILEO GALILEI

GUIDELINES

⋆ for pairing ⋆

WiNe & FOOD

Here are some basic guidelines to making the right decisions when combining wine with food. The key is balance—balancing heavy foods with rich wines, moderate foods with medium-bodied wines, lighter foods with light wines, and sweet foods with sweet wines. Also look for complementary or contrasting flavors to make an impression on your palate (think blue cheese and Port). Ultimately pairing wine with food comes down to your individual tastes, but here are a few tips, hints, ideas, and thoughts.

- ★ **MATCH RICH FOODS WITH RICH FULL-BODIED WINES.** A richly flavored dish with heavy sauces or savory ingredients needs a wine of equal power and flavor. Drink Cabernet Sauvignon with your beef fillet or lamb.

- ★ **SWEET FOODS NEED A SWEET WINE.** A sweet sauce or dessert will cancel out the sweetness in the wine. How about a late-harvest Viognier or Riesling with your crème brûlée?

- ★ **SALTY FOODS NEED A STRONG, FRUIT-FORWARD WINE FOR BALANCE.** Try a high-acidity Sauvignon Blanc with some fruitiness and sweetness for those oysters, or better yet crack open a bottle of sparkling wine.

- ★ **TART FOOD CANCELS OUT A WINE'S FRUITINESS.** Serve slightly sweet and very fruity full-bodied wines with your veal piccata. A crisp Chardonnay or Pinot Blanc would be very nice indeed.

- ★ **FISH NEEDS A MEDIUM-BODIED WINE FOR BALANCE.** Fish can be tricky, as it can be prepared mild or otherwise. Don't be afraid to try a Pinot or other light-bodied red with your salmon. Rich sauces require richer wines.

- ★ **POULTRY CAN THRIVE WITH MANY A BOTTLE.** Depending on its preparation, a soft Viognier, a rich Chardonnay, or a medium Merlot all can work.

- ★ **SPICY AND HOT FOODS ENJOY THE COMPANY OF LIGHTLY SWEET, FRUITY WINES WITH LOW TANNINS.** Enjoy that Thai dish with a Gewürztraminer or a Riesling.

- ★ **SMOKED FOODS OVERPOWER ALL BUT THE FRUITIEST AND RICHEST WINES.** Try a low-tannin rich Merlot with your duck.

FOOD & WINE. DECIDE WHICH IS THE SOLOIST, WHICH THE ACCOMPANIST.

–Michael Broadbent

★ PAIRING ★
FOOD & WINE

CLASSIC WHITE WINE FOOD PAIRINGS

GRAPE	TASTING NOTES
CHARDONNAY	scallops, halibut, shrimp, crab, veal, seafood with butter sauce, chicken, pork, pasta with cream sauce, turkey, ham, pesto, Emmental, Gruyère, Port-Salut, feta, apples, potatoes, squash, mango
RIESLING	mild cheese, clams, mussels, Asian dishes, sashimi, ham, pork, lobster Newberg, tandoori chicken, coquilles Saint-Jacques
SAUVIGNON BLANC	oysters, chicken, turkey, pine nuts, vegetables, grilled or poached salmon, seafood salad, Irish stew, ham, chèvre (goat cheese) and other strongly flavored cheeses, light sauces, quiche, scallops, sorbet, key lime pie
GEWÜRZTRAMINER	spicy dishes, Thai food, curry, smoked salmon, pork and sauerkraut, Muenster, spiced/peppered cheeses, onion tart

CLASSIC RED WINE FOOD PAIRINGS

GRAPE	TASTING NOTES
CABERNET SAUVIGNON	duck, spicy beef, pâté, rabbit, venison, roasts, spicy poultry, cheddar, blue cheese, Gorgonzola, walnuts, sausage, kidneys, broccoli, tomatoes, grilled tuna, tomato sauce, bittersweet chocolate, gelato
PINOT NOIR	braised chicken, cold duck, rabbit, charcuterie, partridge, roast turkey, roast beef, lamb, veal, truffles, Gruyère
MERLOT	braised chicken, cold duck, roast turkey, roast beef, lamb, veal, stew, liver, venison, meat casseroles, Parmesan and Romano cheeses, grilled meats, caramelized onions, béarnaise sauce, dark chocolate, berries, fondue
SYRAH	braised chicken, chili, goose, meat stew, peppercorn steak, barbecued meat, spicy meats, garlic casserole, ratatouille
ZINFANDEL	barbecue, pizza, ribs, sausage, meatloaf, hamburgers, lamb, game, duck, and beef, mildly spiced shellfish and mildly spiced Mexican, Asian and Cajun food, most cheeses, and—of course—chocolate cake

★ PAIRING ★
CHEESE & WINE

Cheese and wine is a classic pairing, but be aware that the common assumption that all wines taste good with cheese can get you into trouble. Some flavorful cheeses can obliterate the wine, making it taste flat and thin. Others are just the right combination. Here is a little background, some guidelines, and some classic combinations.

Since wines do come in a few thousand variations of sweetness, acidity, body, flavor, smell, color, and everything else, you should test recommendations ahead of any big shindig where you are displaying your gastronomical chops. Don't let this hold you back, though, because this is part of the joy of wine-and-food pairing. And remember that *you* are the ultimate gourmet as to what you like. A few guidelines to keep in mind:

★ White wines are best with soft cheeses with stronger flavors.

★ Red wines match best with hard cheeses and milder flavors.

★ Fruity, sweet white wines and dessert wines work with many cheeses.

★ The more pungent the cheese you choose, the sweeter the wine should be.

There are of course hundreds or even thousands of types of cheeses (a cheese cart at even a modest Parisian restaurant will prove that) and thousands of wines. Think of the possibilities and stick to the guidelines, but always eat and drink what *you* like.

A SAMPLING OF CLASSIC CHEESE PAIRINGS

CHEESE	RECOMMENDED WINE
BLUE CHEESE	Cabernet Sauvignon, Zinfandel, a tawny Port, and Sherry
CAMEMBERT OR BRIE	Chardonnay and Sauvignon Blanc
CAHILL (PORTER)	light, fruity reds like Pinot Noir
CHEDDAR	Merlot or Cabernet Sauvignon
CHÈVRE	Gewürztraminer or Champagne
FONTINA	medium-bodied Barberas or Nebbiolos
FETA	dry Chenin Blanc, Sauvignon Blanc, or Pinot Gris for whites, or Pinot Noir for a medium-bodied red
GORGONZOLA	sweet Riesling, Cabernet Sauvignon, or a richly flavored Zinfandel
GOUDA	Riesling and even sparkling wines
GRUYÈRE	Pinot Noir
JARLSBERG	Sauvignon Blanc, Viognier, and light-bodied reds
MONTEREY JACK	Riesling
ROQUEFORT	late-harvest Riesling
STILTON	Port or late-harvest Zinfandel or Cabernet
SWISS	Pinot Noir

★ WINE ★
GLOSSARY

ACID: A key element of wine present in all grapes. When acid is balanced, wine is fresh and has a long life. Wines low in acidity taste flabby.

AGE: The process of maturing in wines. As white wines age, they turn to a golden amber color. Reds usually begin with a purple tone, turning to a deep, brick red color depending on the grape.

ALCOHOL: Alcohol is the natural by-product of fermentation. It is one of the main components of taste along with acids, residual sugar, and tannin.

AMERICAN VITICULTURAL AREA (AVA): When an AVA is designated on a wine label, 85 percent of the grapes used to make that wine must have come from that AVA. If a non-AVA appellation or region is designated on a wine label, at least 75 percent of the grapes must come from that area.

ANTHOCYANIN: One of the phenolics present in wine is the red and blue pigments found in the skins of dark grape varieties.

AROMA: What gives a wine its distinctive "nose" or "bouquet."

APPELLATION (AP-PEL-AY-SHUN): The region where a specific grape is grown. Geography and climate combine to produce flavors and style characteristics, which are unique to a region.

ASTRINGENT: High tannic acid content in wine produces this furry, mouth-puckering sensation.

BOUQUET (BOO-KAY): The combination of aromas from wine generally including the more complex scents of bottle-aged wine.

BALANCE: When all elements of a wine are in harmony, with no single element dominating. Acid is balanced against the sweetness, fruit is in balance with oak and tannin, and alcohol is balanced against both acidity and flavor.

BLENDING: The art of mixing different wines to create a better overall wine.

BLIND TASTING: Tasting wine from bottles with their labels hidden.

BOTTLE-AGING: Maturing a wine in the bottle as opposed to a tank or barrel. Some wines may improve in the bottle for ten or more years.

BREATHE: When wine is poured from the bottle into another container, such as a wineglass or carafe, it mixes with air, releasing aromas, which become more pronounced as time passes. Well-made, young wines will improve and "open up" with an hour or more to breathe.

BUTTERY: The flavor of a white wine that has gone through malolactic fermentation; usually found in Chardonnay.

CORKED: A cork may become contaminated with the chemical compound TCA (2,4,6-trichloroanisole) and impart the taste of cork on the wine. Screw caps and synthetic corks have fewer TCA contamination problems.

CREAMY: Refers to the silky taste of wines, usually white, that are subjected to malolactic fermentation, as opposed to the tart or crisp flavors found in wines that are made without this process.

CRISP: A term used when wine has a pronounced but pleasing tartness or acidity. Generally used to describe white wine.

CUVÉE (COO-VAY): A term for the initial pressing of the grapes. Also a term for a blend of high-quality wines.

DECANTING: Pouring wine slowly from the bottle into a carafe, which adds oxygen and separates the wine from the sediment.

CASE: Twelve 750-ml bottles of wine.

CEDAR: The term denoting the woody aromas found in red wines.

CHAMBRER: A term describing opening a bottle of wine so it can come into contact with the air and reach room temperature. From the French, meaning "allow to breathe."

CITRUSY: An aroma and flavor of citrus, often grapefruit, generally found in white wines made from grapes grown in cooler regions of California.

CLARIFICATION: The process of clearing a wine that involves binding cloudy substances and particles, which then settle on the bottom, becoming sediment.

CLONE: The offspring of grape vines that contains the genetic material of the parent. There are many clones with different characteristics for each grape variety.

CLOUDY: Opposite of clear; considered to be a fault in wine.

COMPLEXITY: When a wine is rich, deep in flavors, nuanced, and well-balanced.

CRUSH: The season when the grapes are harvested and made into wine.

DRY: A term meaning the lack of sweetness in a wine.

ENOLOGY: The science of wine production. Also spelled *oenology*.

FERMENTATION: The process of winemaking that turns the sugar in the grapes into alcohol and carbon dioxide.

FINING: The process of clearing a wine that involves binding cloudy particles, which then settle and become sediment. Same as clarification.

FLAT: A wine-tasting term denoting very low acid and lack of flavor.

FLAVONE: One of the phenolics found in wine; the yellow pigment in small amounts in all pale and dark-skinned grape varieties.

FLINTY: A stone or mineral-like character used often to describe French Chablis and Sauvignon Blanc.

FLORAL: A wine-tasting term indicating the aroma or taste of flowers, mostly used to describe white wines.

FORWARD: Wine-tasting term describing the fruitiness in a wine; it indicates that the wine is ready to drink.

FRENCH OAK: The classic wood flavors of vanilla and cedar that come from wine stored in wood barrels. Different French forests impart slightly different characteristics to the wine.

FRESH: Describes the lively fruity acidity of a good young wine.

FULL-BODIED: A wine-tasting term denoting a wine that fills the mouth and palate.

GLYCERIN: A natural by-product of the fermentation process, giving wine a sweet taste on the tongue and a smooth sensation in the mouth.

GRASSY: The taste of fresh hay frequently found in Sauvignon Blanc.

HERBACEOUS: The smell or taste of herbs found in Cabernet Sauvignon and Sauvignon Blanc.

LATE HARVEST: Describes wines made from grapes harvested later than normal and consequently having higher sugar levels.

LEES: The sediment remaining in the tank or barrel after fermentation.

LEGS: Swirling a wineglass filled with wine will produce rivulets, arches, or legs.

MACERATION: Part of the fermentation process where grape skins, seeds, and stems are steeped for hours or weeks before pressing. The process extracts color, tannin, and aroma into the must.

MADERIZED: A wine that shows signs of oxidation, including a brown color and stinky nose.

MASH: The pulp of the grape, including skins and seeds, that settles in a fermentation tank or barrel.

MERITAGE: Combining the words *merit* and *heritage*, a blend made from several varieties of quality grapes, usually the Bordeaux varietals: Cabernet Sauvignon, Merlot, Cabernet Franc, Petite Verdot, and Malbec.

MÉTHODE CHAMPENOISE: The time-consuming, secondary fermentation process that takes place inside the bottle to create sparkling wine. Developed in the Champagne region of France.

MUST: Raw, unfermented grape juice.

NOBLE ROT: *Botrytis cinerea*. A fungus or mold that causes grapes to shrivel and the grape sugars and acids to become concentrated. Excellent honey-flavored dessert wines are made from these grapes.

NONVINTAGE: A blend of multiple harvests.

NOSE: The overall scent of a wine.

NOUVEAU: A tradition in the Beaujolais region of France, where wines are fermented quickly, bottled, and rushed to market for the fall and winter holidays.

OENOLOGY: The science of wine production. Also spelled *enology*.

OXIDATION: The result of too much oxygen in the wine, causing color change and loss of freshness.

PH VALUE: A chemical measurement of the intensity of acidity in a wine. Low pH wines have more intense acids and are better candidates for aging.

PHENOLICS: Substances extracted from grape skins that provide the color and texture for red wine, specifically, anthocyanins, flavones, and tannins.

PRESSING: The process that separates the grape solids from the juice.

PUNT: The name of the indentation found in the bottom of many wine bottles.

RACKING: A natural and less disturbing clarification process that removes sediment by transferring the wine from one container to another until it is clear.

RESIDUAL SUGAR: The natural sweetness of a wine, produced from the sugar not converted to alcohol during fermentation. Dry wines have little or no residual sugar while dessert wines can have 10 percent or more.

ROSÉ: Pink wine, usually fruity and made from black grapes with little skin contact or from a blend of red and white wines.

SEDIMENT: The accumulation of tannins and pigment deposits in a bottle of wine. It can be removed by decanting.

SOLERA: System for making Brandies, Sherry, Port, and other fortified wines that ensures the same quality year after year.

SOMMELIER (SOH-MEL-LEE-AY): French term for a professional wine server.

STABILIZATION: A condition after fermentation when the wine has all the undesirable sediment removed and appears clear in the bottle.

SULFITES: A derivative of sulfur and natural by-product of fermentation. Also used to clean and sterilize wine-making equipment and to prevent wine from browning. Wines with more than 10 parts per million must state "contains sulfites" on the label.

TANNIN: Provides the astringent mouth-puckering effect in wines that is important in the aging of red wines. Tannin decreases as wine ages, allowing the more subtle flavors of the wine to emerge.

TARTRATES: The natural and harmless crystals that often form in barrels, bottles, and on the cork. The safe glasslike deposits are from tartaric acids present in the wine.

TASTE: Four basic tastes detected by the tongue—sweet, salty, sour, and bitter.

VARIETAL (VAH-RYE-AH-TALL): The grape variety used to make wine. In Europe, wines are usually named after the region in which the grapes are grown (e.g., Bordeaux, Chianti, Burgundy). Elsewhere, wines are usually labeled with the name of the grape variety that the wine is made from (e.g., Cabernet, Chardonnay).

VEGETAL: The smell or taste of green vegetables that can detract from a wine's taste if too intense.

VÉRAISON (VE-RAY-ZON): When the red grapes turn color and white grapes become translucent. This is the phase of growth when the sugar begins to form.

VINIFICATION: The production of wine from the harvest to the bottling.

VINTAGE: A term referring to the year in which the grapes were grown. Also can denote a wine from an exceptional year.

VINTAGE DATE: Refers to the year the grapes were harvested. Most wine regions require that at least 95 percent of the wine contain grapes harvested from that year.

VITICULTURE: The science of growing grapes.

WINE-TASTING: Considering how soil, climate, and weather affect different varieties of grapes, and how these factors are manifested in the taste of the wine. Wine-tasting breaks down into four basic steps:

1. Color and clarity of the wine
2. Smell, which is referred to as aroma or "the nose"
3. Taste
4. Aftertaste

Tasters use specific words and phrases such as "buttery," "cedar," "crisp," "creamy," and "bright" to describe their perceptions of the wine. These words and phrases describe the subtle flavors of the wines that differentiate one from the next.

YEAST: Microorganisms responsible for fermentation—converting sugar to alcohol and carbon dioxide. Yeasts naturally occur on grape skins though most winemakers use cultured yeasts for winemaking.

YIELD: The amount of grapes produced from a particular vineyard.

tasting notes

....

....

....

....   ★ DATE ★

....

....   ★ NAME ★

....

....

....   ★ VARIETAL ★

....

....

....   ★ VINTAGE ★

....

....   ★ REGION ★

....

....

....   ★ PRICE ★

....

....

....

....

....

tasting notes

....

....

....

★ DATE ★

....

....

....

★ NAME ★

....

....

....

....

....

★ VARIETAL ★

....

....

....

....

★ VINTAGE ★

....

....

....

★ REGION ★

....

....

....

★ PRICE ★

....

....

....

....

....

....

tasting notes

....
....
....
....   ★ DATE ★
....
....   ★ NAME ★
....
....
....
....   ★ VARIETAL ★
....
....
....   ★ VINTAGE ★
....
....   ★ REGION ★
....
....
....   ★ PRICE ★
....
....
....
....
....

tasting notes

....

....

....

★ DATE ★

....

★ NAME ★

....

....

....

★ VARIETAL ★

....

....

★ VINTAGE ★

....

★ REGION ★

....

....

★ PRICE ★

....

....

....

....

....

....

....

....

....

....

....

....

....

....

....

tasting notes

....

....

....

....

....   ★ DATE ★

....

....   ★ NAME ★

....

....

....

....   ★ VARIETAL ★

....

....

....   ★ VINTAGE ★

....

....   ★ REGION ★

....

....

....   ★ PRICE ★

....

....

....

....

....

tasting notes

....

....

....

★ DATE ★

....

....
★ NAME ★

....

....

....

....

....
★ VARIETAL ★

....

....

....

....

★ VINTAGE ★

....

....

★ REGION ★

....

....

....

....

★ PRICE ★

....

....

....

....

....

tasting notes

....

....

....

....

.... ★ DATE ★

....

.... ★ NAME ★

....

....

....

.... ★ VARIETAL ★

....

....

.... ★ VINTAGE ★

....

.... ★ REGION ★

....

....

.... ★ PRICE ★

....

....

....

....

....

IN VICTORY, YOU DESERVE CHAMPAGNE; IN DEFEAT, YOU NEED IT.

-NAPOLÉON BONAPARTE

tasting notes

....

....

....

....   ★ DATE ★

....

....   ★ NAME ★

....

....

....

....   ★ VARIETAL ★

....

....

....   ★ VINTAGE ★

....

....   ★ REGION ★

....

....

....   ★ PRICE ★

....

....

....

....

....

tasting notes

....

....

....

★ DATE ★

....

....

★ NAME ★

....

....

....

....

....

★ VARIETAL ★

....

....

....

....

★ VINTAGE ★

....

....

★ REGION ★

....

....

....

....

....

★ PRICE ★

....

....

....

....

....

tasting notes

....
....
....
....

★ DATE ★

....
....
....

★ NAME ★

....
....
....
....
....
....

★ VARIETAL ★

....
....
....
....

★ VINTAGE ★

....
....

★ REGION ★

....
....
....
....

★ PRICE ★

....
....
....
....
....

tasting notes

....

....

....

★ DATE ★

....

....

....

★ NAME ★

....

....

....

....

....

★ VARIETAL ★

....

....

....

....

....

★ VINTAGE ★

....

....

....

★ REGION ★

....

....

....

....

....

★ PRICE ★

....

....

....

....

....

....

tasting notes

....
....
....
....

★ DATE ★

....
....

★ NAME ★

....
....

....
....

....

★ VARIETAL ★

....
....

....

★ VINTAGE ★

....
....

★ REGION ★

....
....

....

★ PRICE ★

....
....

....
....

tasting notes

★ DATE ★

★ NAME ★

★ VARIETAL ★

★ VINTAGE ★

★ REGION ★

★ PRICE ★

tasting notes

....
....
....
....

★ DATE ★

....
....
★ NAME ★

....
....
....
....
....
....
★ VARIETAL ★

....
....
....
....
★ VINTAGE ★

....
....
★ REGION ★

....
....
....
....
★ PRICE ★

....
....
....
....
....

tasting notes

....

....

....

★ DATE ★

....

★ NAME ★

....

....

....

★ VARIETAL ★

....

....

★ VINTAGE ★

....

★ REGION ★

....

....

★ PRICE ★

....

....

....

....

....

....

....

....

....

....

....

....

....

....

....

....

tasting notes

★ DATE ★

★ NAME ★

★ VARIETAL ★

★ VINTAGE ★

★ REGION ★

★ PRICE ★

tasting notes

★ DATE ★

★ NAME ★

★ VARIETAL ★

★ VINTAGE ★

★ REGION ★

★ PRICE ★

tasting notes

....
....
....
....
....   ★ DATE ★
....
....   ★ NAME ★
....
....
....
....   ★ VARIETAL ★
....
....
....   ★ VINTAGE ★
....
....   ★ REGION ★
....
....
....   ★ PRICE ★
....
....
....
....
....

tasting notes

....

....

....

★ DATE ★

....

★ NAME ★

....

....

★ VARIETAL ★

....

....

★ VINTAGE ★

....

★ REGION ★

....

....

★ PRICE ★

....

tasting notes

....
....
....
....   ★ DATE ★
....
....   ★ NAME ★
....
....
....
....   ★ VARIETAL ★
....
....
....   ★ VINTAGE ★
....
....   ★ REGION ★
....
....
....   ★ PRICE ★
....
....
....
....
....

tasting notes

....

....

....

★ DATE ★

....

....

★ NAME ★

....

....

....

....

....

★ VARIETAL ★

....

....

....

....

....

★ VINTAGE ★

....

....

....

★ REGION ★

....

....

....

....

....

★ PRICE ★

....

....

....

....

....

....

WINE
CHEERS THE
SAD, ★
REVIVES THE
OLD, ★
INSPIRES THE
YOUNG,
MAKES WEARINESS FORGET HIS TOIL.
—LORD BYRON

tasting notes

....

....

....

★ DATE ★

....

....

★ NAME ★

....

....

....

....

....

★ VARIETAL ★

....

....

....

....

★ VINTAGE ★

....

....

....

★ REGION ★

....

....

....

....

....

★ PRICE ★

....

....

....

....

....

....

tasting notes

....

....

....

....   ★ DATE ★

....

....   ★ NAME ★

....

....

....

....   ★ VARIETAL ★

....

....

....   ★ VINTAGE ★

....

....   ★ REGION ★

....

....

....   ★ PRICE ★

....

....

....

....

tasting notes

....

....

....

★ DATE ★

....

....

★ NAME ★

....

....

....

....

....

★ VARIETAL ★

....

....

....

....

★ VINTAGE ★

....

....

★ REGION ★

....

....

....

....

★ PRICE ★

....

....

....

....

....

tasting notes

....
....
....
....
....

★ DATE ★

....
....

★ NAME ★

....
....
....
....

★ VARIETAL ★

....
....
....

★ VINTAGE ★

....
....

★ REGION ★

....
....
....

★ PRICE ★

....
....
....
....
....

tasting notes

....

....

....

★ DATE ★

....

★ NAME ★

....

....

★ VARIETAL ★

....

....

★ VINTAGE ★

....

★ REGION ★

....

....

★ PRICE ★

....

tasting notes

....
....
....
....
....

★ DATE ★

....

★ NAME ★

....

....

....

★ VARIETAL ★

....

....

★ VINTAGE ★

....

★ REGION ★

....

....

★ PRICE ★

....

tasting notes

....

....

....

★ DATE ★

....
....

★ NAME ★

....
....

....
....

....

★ VARIETAL ★

....
....

....
....

★ VINTAGE ★

....
....

★ REGION ★

....
....

....
....

★ PRICE ★

....
....

....

....

....

....

tasting notes

....
....
....
....   ★ DATE ★
....
....
....   ★ NAME ★
....
....
....
....
....   ★ VARIETAL ★
....
....
....
....
....   ★ VINTAGE ★
....
....
....   ★ REGION ★
....
....
....
....
....   ★ PRICE ★
....
....
....
....
....
....
....

tasting notes

....

....

....

★ DATE ★   ....

....

★ NAME ★   ....

....

....

★ VARIETAL ★   ....

....

....

★ VINTAGE ★   ....

....

★ REGION ★   ....

....

....

★ PRICE ★   ....

....

....

....

....

tasting notes

....
....
....
....   ★ DATE ★
....
....   ★ NAME ★
....
....
....
....   ★ VARIETAL ★
....
....
....   ★ VINTAGE ★
....
....   ★ REGION ★
....
....
....   ★ PRICE ★
....
....
....
....
....

tasting notes

....

....

....

★ DATE ★

....

★ NAME ★

....

....

★ VARIETAL ★

....

....

★ VINTAGE ★

....

★ REGION ★

....

....

★ PRICE ★

....

....

....

....

....

tasting notes

....

....

....

....   ★ DATE ★

....

....   ★ NAME ★

....

....

....

....   ★ VARIETAL ★

....

....

....   ★ VINTAGE ★

....

....   ★ REGION ★

....

....

....   ★ PRICE ★

....

....

....

....

tasting notes

....

....

....

★ DATE ★

....

....

★ NAME ★

....

....

....

....

....

★ VARIETAL ★

....

....

....

....

★ VINTAGE ★

....

....

....

★ REGION ★

....

....

....

....

....

★ PRICE ★

....

....

....

....

....

....

tasting notes

....

....

....

....

....

★ DATE ★

....

....

★ NAME ★

....

....

....

....

....

★ VARIETAL ★

....

....

....

....

★ VINTAGE ★

....

....

★ REGION ★

....

....

....

....

★ PRICE ★

....

....

....

....

....

THE HISTORY OF
A WINE
IS OF GREATER
MOMENT
THAN THE DISCOVERY OF A
CONSTELLATION.
THE UNIVERSE IS TOO FULL OF STARS.
—BENJAMIN FRANKLIN

....

....

....

....   ★ DATE ★
....
....
....   ★ NAME ★
....
....
....
....
....   ★ VARIETAL ★
....
....
....
....   ★ VINTAGE ★
....
....   ★ REGION ★
....
....
....   ★ PRICE ★
....
....
....
....
....

tasting notes

....

....

....

★ DATE ★

....

★ NAME ★

....

....

★ VARIETAL ★

....

....

★ VINTAGE ★

....

★ REGION ★

....

....

★ PRICE ★

....

tasting notes

....
....
....
....
....   ★ DATE ★
....
....   ★ NAME ★
....
....
....
....   ★ VARIETAL ★
....
....
....   ★ VINTAGE ★
....
....   ★ REGION ★
....
....
....   ★ PRICE ★
....
....
....
....

tasting notes

....

....

....

★ DATE ★

....

....

★ NAME ★

....

....

....

....

....

★ VARIETAL ★

....

....

....

....

....

★ VINTAGE ★

....

....

....

★ REGION ★

....

....

....

....

....

★ PRICE ★

....

....

....

....

....

....

tasting notes

....

....

....

....

....   ★ DATE ★

....

....   ★ NAME ★

....

....

....

....   ★ VARIETAL ★

....

....

....   ★ VINTAGE ★

....

....   ★ REGION ★

....

....

....   ★ PRICE ★

....

....

....

....

....

tasting notes

....

....

....

★ DATE ★

....

....

★ NAME ★

....

....

....

....

....

★ VARIETAL ★

....

....

....

....

★ VINTAGE ★

....

....

....

★ REGION ★

....

....

....

....

★ PRICE ★

....

....

....

....

....

....

....

....

.... ★ DATE ★

....

.... ★ NAME ★

....

....

....

.... ★ VARIETAL ★

....

....

.... ★ VINTAGE ★

....

.... ★ REGION ★

....

....

.... ★ PRICE ★

....

....

....

....

....

tasting notes

....

....

....

★ DATE ★

....

....

★ NAME ★

....

....

....

....

....

★ VARIETAL ★

....

....

....

....

....

★ VINTAGE ★

....

....

....

★ REGION ★

....

....

....

....

....

★ PRICE ★

....

....

....

....

....

....

tasting notes

....
....
....

★ DATE ★

....
....

★ NAME ★

....
....
....

★ VARIETAL ★

....
....

★ VINTAGE ★

....

★ REGION ★

....
....

★ PRICE ★

....
....
....
....
....

tasting notes

....

....

....

★ DATE ★
....

....

★ NAME ★
....

....

....
....

....

★ VARIETAL ★
....

....

....
....

★ VINTAGE ★
....

....

★ REGION ★
....

....

....
....

★ PRICE ★
....

....

....

....

....

tasting notes

....

....

....

....

....

....

....

....

....

....

....

....

....

....

....

....

....

....

....

....

....

....

★ DATE ★

....

★ NAME ★

....

....

★ VARIETAL ★

....

....

★ VINTAGE ★

....

★ REGION ★

....

....

★ PRICE ★

....

tasting notes

....

....

....

★ DATE ★

....

★ NAME ★

....

....

....

★ VARIETAL ★

....

....

★ VINTAGE ★

....

★ REGION ★

....

....

★ PRICE ★

....

....

....

....

tasting notes

....

....

....

....   ★ DATE ★

....

....   ★ NAME ★

....

....

....

....   ★ VARIETAL ★

....

....

....   ★ VINTAGE ★

....

....   ★ REGION ★

....

....

....   ★ PRICE ★

....

....

....

....

....

tasting notes

....

....

....

★ DATE ★

....

★ NAME ★

....

....

★ VARIETAL ★

....

....

★ VINTAGE ★

....

★ REGION ★

....

....

★ PRICE ★

....

....

....

....

THREE

BE THE THINGS

I SHALL NEVER ATTAIN:

ENVY, CONTENT,

AND SUFFICIENT

CHAMPAGNE.

—DOROTHY PARKER

tasting notes

....

....

....

★ DATE ★

....

★ NAME ★

....

....

....

★ VARIETAL ★

....

....

★ VINTAGE ★

....

★ REGION ★

....

....

★ PRICE ★

....

tasting notes

....

....

....

....

....   ★ DATE ★

....

....   ★ NAME ★

....

....

....

....   ★ VARIETAL ★

....

....

....   ★ VINTAGE ★

....

....   ★ REGION ★

....

....

....   ★ PRICE ★

....

....

....

....

tasting notes

....

....

....

★ DATE ★

....

★ NAME ★

....

....

....

★ VARIETAL ★

....

....

★ VINTAGE ★

....

★ REGION ★

....

....

★ PRICE ★

....

....

....

....

tasting notes

....
....
....
....

★ DATE ★

....

★ NAME ★

....
....
....

★ VARIETAL ★

....
....

★ VINTAGE ★

....

★ REGION ★

....
....

★ PRICE ★

....
....
....
....
....
....

tasting notes

....

....

....

★ DATE ★

....

★ NAME ★

....

....

★ VARIETAL ★

....

....

★ VINTAGE ★

....

★ REGION ★

....

....

★ PRICE ★

....

....

....

....

tasting notes

....
....
....
....

★ DATE ★

....
....

★ NAME ★

....
....
....
....

★ VARIETAL ★

....
....

★ VINTAGE ★

....

★ REGION ★

....
....

★ PRICE ★

....
....
....
....

tasting notes

....

....

....

★ DATE ★

....

....

★ NAME ★

....

....

....

....

....

★ VARIETAL ★

....

....

....

....

★ VINTAGE ★

....

....

★ REGION ★

....

....

....

....

★ PRICE ★

....

....

....

....

....

tasting notes

....
....
....
....   ★ DATE ★
....
....   ★ NAME ★
....
....
....
....   ★ VARIETAL ★
....
....
....   ★ VINTAGE ★
....
....   ★ REGION ★
....
....
....   ★ PRICE ★
....
....
....
....

tasting notes

★ DATE ★

★ NAME ★

★ VARIETAL ★

★ VINTAGE ★

★ REGION ★

★ PRICE ★

tasting notes

....
....
....
....

★ DATE ★

....
....

★ NAME ★

....
....

....
....

....

★ VARIETAL ★

....
....

....

★ VINTAGE ★

....
....

....

★ REGION ★

....
....

....

★ PRICE ★

....
....

....
....
....

tasting notes

....

....

....

★ DATE ★

....

....

★ NAME ★

....

....

....

★ VARIETAL ★

....

....

★ VINTAGE ★

....

★ REGION ★

....

....

★ PRICE ★

....

....

....

....

tasting notes

★ DATE ★

★ NAME ★

★ VARIETAL ★

★ VINTAGE ★

★ REGION ★

★ PRICE ★

tasting notes

....

....

....

★ DATE ★

....

★ NAME ★

....

....

★ VARIETAL ★

....

....

★ VINTAGE ★

....

★ REGION ★

....

....

★ PRICE ★

....

tasting notes

....
....
....
....   ★ DATE ★
....
....   ★ NAME ★
....
....
....
....   ★ VARIETAL ★
....
....
....   ★ VINTAGE ★
....
....   ★ REGION ★
....
....
....   ★ PRICE ★
....
....
....
....
....

WINE,

ONE

SIP

OF THIS WILL

BATHE

THE DROOPING

SPIRITS

IN DELIGHT BEYOND THE

BLISS

OF DREAMS. BE WISE AND TASTE.

—JOHN MILTON

tasting notes

....
....
....
....
....   ★ DATE ★
....
....   ★ NAME ★
....
....
....
....   ★ VARIETAL ★
....
....
....   ★ VINTAGE ★
....
....   ★ REGION ★
....
....
....   ★ PRICE ★
....
....
....
....
....

★ DATE ★

★ NAME ★

★ VARIETAL ★

★ VINTAGE ★

★ REGION ★

★ PRICE ★

tasting notes

....

....

....

....

....

....

....

....

....

....

....

....

....

....

....

....

....

....

....

tasting notes

....

....

....

....   ★ DATE ★

....

....   ★ NAME ★

....

....

....   ★ VARIETAL ★

....

....

....   ★ VINTAGE ★

....

....   ★ REGION ★

....

....

....   ★ PRICE ★

....

....

....

....

tasting notes

....

....

....

★ DATE ★

....

★ NAME ★

....

....

....

★ VARIETAL ★

....

....

★ VINTAGE ★

....

★ REGION ★

....

....

★ PRICE ★

....

....

....

....

tasting notes

....

....

....

....   ★ DATE ★

....

....   ★ NAME ★

....

....

....

....   ★ VARIETAL ★

....

....

....   ★ VINTAGE ★

....

....   ★ REGION ★

....

....

....   ★ PRICE ★

....

....

....

....

....

tasting notes

....

....

....

★ DATE ★   ....

....

★ NAME ★   ....

....

....

....

★ VARIETAL ★   ....

....

....

★ VINTAGE ★   ....

....

★ REGION ★   ....

....

....

★ PRICE ★   ....

....

....

....

....

tasting notes

★ DATE ★

★ NAME ★

★ VARIETAL ★

★ VINTAGE ★

★ REGION ★

★ PRICE ★

tasting notes

....

....

....

★ DATE ★

....

....

★ NAME ★

....

....

....

....

....

★ VARIETAL ★

....

....

....

★ VINTAGE ★

....

....

★ REGION ★

....

....

....

....

★ PRICE ★

....

....

....

....

....

tasting notes

★ DATE ★

★ NAME ★

★ VARIETAL ★

★ VINTAGE ★

★ REGION ★

★ PRICE ★

★ DATE ★

★ NAME ★

★ VARIETAL ★

★ VINTAGE ★

★ REGION ★

★ PRICE ★

tasting notes

tasting notes

....
....
....
....
....   ★ DATE ★
....
....   ★ NAME ★
....
....
....
....   ★ VARIETAL ★
....
....
....   ★ VINTAGE ★
....
....   ★ REGION ★
....
....
....   ★ PRICE ★
....
....
....
....
....
....

tasting notes

....

....

....

★ DATE ★
....

....
....

★ NAME ★
....

....
....

....
....

....
....

★ VARIETAL ★
....

....
....

....
....

★ VINTAGE ★
....

....
....

★ REGION ★
....

....
....

....
....

★ PRICE ★
....

....
....

....

....

....

tasting notes

....
....
....
....
....

★ DATE ★

....
....

★ NAME ★

....
....

....
....

....
....

★ VARIETAL ★

....
....

....
....

★ VINTAGE ★

....
....

....

★ REGION ★

....
....

....
....

★ PRICE ★

....
....

....
....
....
....

tasting notes

....
....
....
★ DATE ★   ....
....
....
★ NAME ★   ....
....
....
....
....
....
★ VARIETAL ★   ....
....
....
....
★ VINTAGE ★   ....
....
....
★ REGION ★   ....
....
....
....
★ PRICE ★   ....
....
....
....
....
....

WINE IS THE MOST

CIVILIZED

THING

IN THE WORLD.

–ERNEST HEMINGWAY

tasting notes

....

....

....

★ DATE ★

....

....

★ NAME ★

....

....

....

....

★ VARIETAL ★

....

....

....

★ VINTAGE ★

....

★ REGION ★

....

....

★ PRICE ★

....

....

....

....

....

tasting notes

....
....
....
....   ★ DATE ★
....
....   ★ NAME ★
....
....
....
....   ★ VARIETAL ★
....
....
....   ★ VINTAGE ★
....
....   ★ REGION ★
....
....
....   ★ PRICE ★
....
....
....
....
....

tasting notes

....
....
....

★ DATE ★

....

....

★ NAME ★

....

....
....

....

★ VARIETAL ★

....

....
....

....

★ VINTAGE ★

....

....

★ REGION ★

....

....
....

....

★ PRICE ★

....

....
....

....

....

tasting notes

....
....
....
....   ★ DATE ★
....
....   ★ NAME ★
....
....
....
....   ★ VARIETAL ★
....
....
....   ★ VINTAGE ★
....
....   ★ REGION ★
....
....
....   ★ PRICE ★
....
....
....
....
....

tasting notes

....

....

....

★ DATE ★
....

....
....

★ NAME ★
....

....
....

....
....

★ VARIETAL ★
....

....
....

....
....

★ VINTAGE ★
....

....
....

★ REGION ★
....

....
....

....
....

★ PRICE ★
....

....
....

....

....

....

tasting notes

....
....
....
....

★ DATE ★

....
....

★ NAME ★

....
....
....
....

★ VARIETAL ★

....
....

★ VINTAGE ★

....

★ REGION ★

....
....

★ PRICE ★

....
....
....
....

tasting notes

....
....
....

★ DATE ★

....

★ NAME ★

....

....

....

★ VARIETAL ★

....

....

★ VINTAGE ★

....

★ REGION ★

....

....

★ PRICE ★

....

....
....
....
....
....
....
....
....
....
....

tasting notes

....

....

....

....   ★ DATE ★

....

....   ★ NAME ★

....

....

....

....   ★ VARIETAL ★

....

....

....   ★ VINTAGE ★

....

....   ★ REGION ★

....

....

....   ★ PRICE ★

....

....

....

....

....

★ DATE ★

★ NAME ★

★ VARIETAL ★

★ VINTAGE ★

★ REGION ★

★ PRICE ★

tasting notes

tasting notes

....
....
....
....
....

★ DATE ★

....

....

★ NAME ★

....

....

....

....

★ VARIETAL ★

....

....

....

....

★ VINTAGE ★

....

....

★ REGION ★

....

....

....

....

★ PRICE ★

....

....

....

....

....

tasting notes

....

....

....

★ DATE ★

....

....

★ NAME ★

....

....

....

....

....

★ VARIETAL ★

....

....

....

....

★ VINTAGE ★

....

....

★ REGION ★

....

....

....

....

....

★ PRICE ★

....

....

....

....

....

....

tasting notes

....
....
....

★ DATE ★

....

★ NAME ★

....

....

....

★ VARIETAL ★

....

....

....   ★ VINTAGE ★

....

....   ★ REGION ★

....

....

....   ★ PRICE ★

....

....
....
....
....

★ DATE ★

★ NAME ★

★ VARIETAL ★

★ VINTAGE ★

★ REGION ★

★ PRICE ★

tasting notes

tasting notes

....

....

....

....

....

....

....

....

....

....

....

....

....

....

....

....

....

....

....

....

★ DATE ★

....

★ NAME ★

....

....

....

★ VARIETAL ★

....

....

★ VINTAGE ★

....

★ REGION ★

....

....

★ PRICE ★

....

the FLAVOR OF WINE IS LIKE DELICATE POETRY.

— LOUIS PASTEUR

tasting notes

....
....
....
....

★ DATE ★

....
....

....

★ NAME ★

....
....

....
....

....
....

....

★ VARIETAL ★

....
....

....
....

....

★ VINTAGE ★

....
....

....

★ REGION ★

....
....

....
....

....

★ PRICE ★

....
....

....
....
....
....

tasting notes

....

....

....

★ DATE ★

....

....

★ NAME ★

....

....

....

....

....

★ VARIETAL ★

....

....

....

....

....

★ VINTAGE ★

....

....

....

★ REGION ★

....

....

....

....

....

★ PRICE ★

....

....

....

....

....

....

tasting notes

....

....

....

....

....   ★ DATE ★

....

....   ★ NAME ★

....

....

....

....   ★ VARIETAL ★

....

....

....   ★ VINTAGE ★

....

....   ★ REGION ★

....

....

....   ★ PRICE ★

....

....

....

....

tasting notes

....

....

....

★ DATE ★

....

★ NAME ★

....

....

....

★ VARIETAL ★

....

....

★ VINTAGE ★

....

★ REGION ★

....

....

★ PRICE ★

....

....

....

....

tasting notes

....
....
....
....   ★ DATE ★
....
....
....   ★ NAME ★
....
....
....
....
....   ★ VARIETAL ★
....
....
....
....
....   ★ VINTAGE ★
....
....
....   ★ REGION ★
....
....
....
....
....
....   ★ PRICE ★
....
....
....
....
....
....
....

tasting notes

....

....

....

★ DATE ★   ....

....

★ NAME ★   ....

....

....

★ VARIETAL ★   ....

....

....

★ VINTAGE ★   ....

....

★ REGION ★   ....

....

....

★ PRICE ★   ....

....

....

....

....

tasting notes

....
....
....
....   ★ DATE ★
                                                                         ....
....   ★ NAME ★
....
....
....
....
....
....   ★ VARIETAL ★
....
....
....
....
....   ★ VINTAGE ★
....
....
....   ★ REGION ★
....
....
....
....
....   ★ PRICE ★
....
....
....
....
....
....

tasting notes

....

....

....

★ DATE ★

....

....

★ NAME ★

....

....

....

....

....

★ VARIETAL ★

....

....

....

....

....

★ VINTAGE ★

....

....

....

★ REGION ★

....

....

....

....

....

★ PRICE ★

....

....

....

....

....

....

tasting notes

....
....
....
....
....   ★ DATE ★
....
....   ★ NAME ★
....
....
....
....   ★ VARIETAL ★
....
....
....   ★ VINTAGE ★
....
....   ★ REGION ★
....
....
....   ★ PRICE ★
....
....
....
....

tasting notes

....

....

....

★ DATE ★

....

★ NAME ★

....

....

....

★ VARIETAL ★

....

....

★ VINTAGE ★

....

★ REGION ★

....

....

★ PRICE ★

....

....

....

....

tasting notes

....
....
....
....

★ DATE ★

....

★ NAME ★

....
....
....

★ VARIETAL ★

....
....

★ VINTAGE ★

....

★ REGION ★

....
....

★ PRICE ★

....
....
....
....
....
....

tasting notes

....

....

....

★ DATE ★   ....

....

★ NAME ★   ....

....

....

★ VARIETAL ★   ....

....

....

★ VINTAGE ★   ....

....

★ REGION ★   ....

....

....

★ PRICE ★   ....

....

....

....

....

tasting notes

....
....
....
....   ★ DATE ★
....
....   ★ NAME ★
....
....
....
....   ★ VARIETAL ★
....
....
....   ★ VINTAGE ★
....
....   ★ REGION ★
....
....
....   ★ PRICE ★
....
....
....
....
....

tasting notes

....

....

....

★ DATE ★

....

....

★ NAME ★

....

....

....

....

....

★ VARIETAL ★

....

....

....

....

★ VINTAGE ★

....

....

★ REGION ★

....

....

....

....

★ PRICE ★

....

....

....

....

....

WINE MAKES

a **MAN MORE PLEASED WITH HIMSELF;** I DO NOT SAY IT MAKES HIM MORE PLEASING TO OTHERS.

−SAMUEL JOHNSON

tasting notes

....

....

....

★ DATE ★

....

....

★ NAME ★

....

....

....

....

....

★ VARIETAL ★

....

....

....

....

★ VINTAGE ★

....

....

★ REGION ★

....

....

....

....

★ PRICE ★

....

....

....

....

....

tasting notes

....

....

....

....   ★ DATE ★

....

....   ★ NAME ★

....

....

....

....   ★ VARIETAL ★

....

....

....   ★ VINTAGE ★

....

....   ★ REGION ★

....

....

....   ★ PRICE ★

....

....

....

....

....

tasting notes

....

....

....

★ DATE ★

....

....

....

★ NAME ★

....

....

....

....

....

★ VARIETAL ★

....

....

....

....

★ VINTAGE ★

....

....

....

★ REGION ★

....

....

....

....

★ PRICE ★

....

....

....

....

....

....

tasting notes

....

....

....

....   ★ DATE ★

....

....   ★ NAME ★

....

....

....

....   ★ VARIETAL ★

....

....

....   ★ VINTAGE ★

....

....   ★ REGION ★

....

....

....   ★ PRICE ★

....

....

....

....

tasting notes

....

....

....

★ DATE ★   ....

....

★ NAME ★   ....

....

....

★ VARIETAL ★   ....

....

....

★ VINTAGE ★   ....

....

★ REGION ★   ....

....

....

★ PRICE ★   ....

....

....

....

....

tasting notes

....
....
....
....

★ DATE ★
....

....

★ NAME ★
....

....
....

....
....

....

★ VARIETAL ★
....

....
....

....

★ VINTAGE ★
....

....

★ REGION ★
....

....
....

....

★ PRICE ★
....

....
....
....
....

tasting notes

....

....

....

★ DATE ★

....

★ NAME ★

....

....

....

★ VARIETAL ★

....

....

★ VINTAGE ★

....

★ REGION ★

....

....

★ PRICE ★

....

....

....

....

tasting notes

....
....
....
....

★ DATE ★

....
....

★ NAME ★

....
....
....
....
....

★ VARIETAL ★

....
....
....

★ VINTAGE ★

....
....

★ REGION ★

....
....
....

★ PRICE ★

....
....
....
....
....

tasting notes

....

....

....

★ DATE ★

....

....

★ NAME ★

....

....

....

....

....

★ VARIETAL ★

....

....

....

....

....

★ VINTAGE ★

....

....

★ REGION ★

....

....

....

....

....

★ PRICE ★

....

....

....

....

....

....

tasting notes

....
....
....
....
....   ★ DATE ★
....
....
....   ★ NAME ★
....
....
....
....
....
....
....   ★ VARIETAL ★
....
....
....
....
....   ★ VINTAGE ★
....
....
....   ★ REGION ★
....
....
....
....
....   ★ PRICE ★
....
....
....
....
....
....

tasting notes

....

....

....

★ DATE ★   ....

....

★ NAME ★   ....

....

....

★ VARIETAL ★   ....

....

....

★ VINTAGE ★   ....

....

★ REGION ★   ....

....

....

★ PRICE ★   ....

....

....

....

....

tasting notes

....
....
....
....   ★ DATE ★
....
....   ★ NAME ★
....
....
....
....   ★ VARIETAL ★
....
....
....   ★ VINTAGE ★
....
....   ★ REGION ★
....
....
....   ★ PRICE ★
....
....
....
....
....

tasting notes

....

....

....

★ DATE ★

....

★ NAME ★

....

....

....

★ VARIETAL ★

....

....

★ VINTAGE ★

....

★ REGION ★

....

....

★ PRICE ★

....

....

....

....

tasting notes

....

....

....

....   ★ DATE ★

....

....   ★ NAME ★

....

....

....

....   ★ VARIETAL ★

....

....

....   ★ VINTAGE ★

....

....   ★ REGION ★

....

....

....   ★ PRICE ★

....

....

....

....

GOOD WINE IS A GOOD FAMILIAR CREATURE IF IT BE WELL USED.

–WILLIAM SHAKESPEARE

tasting notes

★ DATE ★

★ NAME ★

★ VARIETAL ★

★ VINTAGE ★

★ REGION ★

★ PRICE ★

WINE BLOGS & WEBSITES WORTH VISITING

BENITO'S WINE REVIEWS (wine-by-benito.blogspot.com): A great food and wine blog from Ben Carter. Let Ben excite your taste buds with great wine and food pairings along with photographs and recipes.

DR. VINO'S WINE BLOG (www.drvino.com): Wine writer and educator Tyler Colman wrote his Ph.D. dissertation on the political economy of the wine industry in France and America and now shares recommendations for wines and wine bars on this blog.

FERMENTATIONS–THE DAILY WINE BLOG (fermentation.typepad.com): Set inside the world of wine public relations. Join Tom Wark and his daily wine discourse.

GOOD GRAPE (goodgrape.com): A free-spirited, "outside the beltway" perspective on the culture and business of wine written for wine enthusiasts who want a peek behind the wine industry's "lifestyle" curtain.

THE POUR (thepour.blogs.nytimes.com): The Pour is about the pleasure of drinking wine, and occasionally beer and spirits, too. It also addresses wine issues and expands on Eric Asimov's columns in the *New York Times*.

THE WINERY ADVISOR (wineryadvisor.wordpress.com): The California Winery Advisor's blog. Learn about new wineries, tasting rooms, and wine country travel throughout California.

VERITAS IN VINO (www.alicefeiring.com): Written by journalist Alice Feiring, who has contributed to the *New York Times* and other publications. Called part of the "real flowering of high-quality wine journalism" by wine columnist Michael Steinberger.

VINOGRAPHY (www.vinography.com): Alder Yarrow writes daily about wines, the wine world, and good restaurants around the globe. *San Francisco* magazine calls Alder "the wine world's brightest cyberstar."